SPARKS

A Selection of Short Bible Devotionals for Reflection or Discussion.

JOHN AVERY

THE SPARKS SERIES

THE SPARKS SERIES

Copyright © John Avery, 2023

All rights reserved.

Without limiting the rights under copyright reserved above, no part of this publication longer than 100 words may be reproduced, stored in or introduced into a retrieval system, or transmitted, in any form, or by any means (electronic, mechanical, photocopying, recording, or otherwise), without the prior written permission of the copyright owner.

Permission is given to quote less than 100 words on condition that the following citation followed by a page number is used in footnotes, endnotes, or adjacent to the quotation: "John Avery, *Sparks*, 2023. Page ***. Used with permission."

ISBN: 978-0-9986507-8-4 (Paperback)
ISBN: 978-0-9986507-9-1 (eBook)

Cover design by Nada Orlic
Formatting by Luca Funari

Scripture quotations taken from the (NASB®) New American Standard Bible®, Copyright © 1960, 1971, 1977, 1995, 2020 by The Lockman Foundation. Used by permission. All rights reserved. *www.lockman.org*.

Many of the pieces in this collection first appeared on *www.BibleMaturity.com* and will appear in other topical compilations by the author.

Contents

The Sparks Series 5

- Director's Cut .... (Matthew 13:10–13) 7
- Peepholes into God .... (Psalm 22:22) 9
- The Blue Touch Paper .... (Matthew 8:2–3) 11
- Scrumping .... (Genesis 3:6) 13
- Spiritual Forensics .... (Acts 4:7–12) 15
- Baby Giants .... (2 Samuel 21:15–17) 17
- Kings and Stars .... (Matthew 2:9) 19
- Live Bait .... (John 8:3–11) 21
- Meet the Magician .... (Acts 8:10) 23
- The Greatest Faith .... (Luke 7:9) 25
- The Revealer of Mysteries .... (Daniel 2:26–28) 27
- Reflections of a Fisher of Men .... (Matthew 4:19) 30
- Belief and Unbelief on a Journey ..... (John 4:48–53) 32
- Footprints on the Ceiling .... (Colossians 3:23–24) 34
- Choose Your Blessing .... (Genesis 27:26–29; 35:9–12) ... 36
- People of Lystra .... (Acts 14:15) 39
- The Hill Country .... (Numbers 13:27–28, 30–31; 14:7–9) ... 41
- Pssst ... Wanna See an Angel? .... (Matthew 4:11; Luke 22:42–43) ... 43
- Betrayal .... (2 Timothy 1:7–8) 45
- The Hall of Faith .... (Hebrews 11:1–2, 8–10) 47
- A Resignation Speech .... (1 Kings 19:4, 9–10) 50

- The Multivitamin Gos-Pill *(Matthew 4:23; 9:35 and more)* 53
- Rhema or Rabbit Trail? *(Luke 5:2–5)* 56
- A Sigh at Sunrise *(Psalm 130:5–6))* 58
- The Grand Themes of Jesus *(Various)* 60
- Earthquake Pre-prayer-edness *(Acts 16:25–28)* 62
- Man in the Spotlight *(Matthew 21:5; John 12:16)* 64
- Kites without Strings *(2 Peter 3:1–2)* 66

About the Author 71

The SPARKS SERIES

The pieces I write are not exactly devotionals though they have some of the flavor of a devotional: they are short enough to be read in a few minutes and can be used daily for a few weeks, each is a reflection on at least one Bible verse, and some life application is encouraged. However, the pieces are designed to stimulate deeper reflection than the average devotional. I think of them as sparks.

Jesus' life and words frequently challenged people's established ways of living. He didn't come to bless life as we know it; He invites us to lay down our old ways and receive His kingdom life instead. When a wildfire rages through brush it quickly consumes the dead and the dry. After the rain, and the space of a few weeks, new life sprouts. I pray that these pieces will be sparks to lives that are surrendered to burning and committed to the slower process of nurturing kingdom ways in place of the old.

My prayer is that a flame would ignite in your brain, fire up your thinking, race to your heart, and jump from the tips of your fingers, toes, and tongue. Feed the flames so that your thoughts turn to passion, and your passion to action. May it be of such intensity that, everywhere you walk, every life that you touch begins to glow in turn.

No fire has value except the fire of the glory of God. The words of the Bible are more important than mine. For the sake of space, I have only included a few verses in each piece (noted on the Contents page). So, please take time to reflect on each Scripture in its context and, if possible, read any parallel accounts (provided under chapter headings). Imagine the scenes and consider the characters. As I read the passages, the Spirit's finger pointed at things in my life and inspired each piece; ask Him to work in your life too. It's His finger that beckons us out of our old ways and points us to the ways of Jesus.

May you burn with His fire as a result of reflecting on these simple sparks, which are a selection from the following topics and are arranged here in no particular order. If you enjoy this little book, look out for other compilations of short pieces in titles or on topics like:

Look out for other compilations of short pieces on topics like:

- *The Questions of Jesus* — Published October 2022
- *The Kingdom of God* — Published March 2023
- Our Identity as Children of God (being like Jesus)
- Conversation with God (commonly called prayer)
- Faith in God
- The Spirit of God
- Following the Voice of God (calling and guidance)
- Revival from God
- Prophets of God
- Names of God
- Followers of Jesus (what it means to be a disciple)
- Kings of Israel (David, Saul, and others)
- Fathers of Faith (Abraham, Jacob, and Moses)

Director's Cut

(Context: Matthew 13:1–23. Parallels: Mark 4:1–20; Luke 8:4–15.)

"The man in the boat was such fun. I loved his stories! He told them so well. What did they say his name was?"

"I forget his name, but you're right, he's great. I especially liked the one about the seeds, and the birds that gobbled most of them up. Let's find out where he's speaking next and arrive early before it gets too crowded. We might even get a free lunch."

Meanwhile, *"the disciples came up and said to Him, 'Why do You speak to [the crowds] in parables?' And Jesus answered them, 'To you it has been granted to know the mysteries of the kingdom of heaven, but to them it has not been granted. For whoever has, to him more shall be given, and he will have an abundance; but whoever does not have, even what he has shall be taken away from him. Therefore I speak to them in parables; because while seeing they do not see, and while hearing they do not hear, nor do they understand.'"* (Matthew 13:10–13)

Jesus had just told His famous parable of parables with its cast and props: pesky birds, vicious thorns, obstructive rocks, and mysterious seeds sown by a nameless sower. It is one of only two parables that Jesus ever explained.

Luke is the most honest. He says that the disciples approached Jesus later. "By the way, Jesus, what did your story actually mean?" Matthew hides their ignorance. Regardless, Jesus explained the plot to His handpicked followers. At first, it seems unfair, even exclusive, that they should get the special edition, the Director's Cut.

But wait, parables are a heart test. Scatter a few carefully chosen words among a crowd and see what responses sprout up. Give it a few minutes and some people will have lost every word to a flock of fluttering distractions. Wait until the crowd faces the mid-week heat of their tough careers and quarrelsome families—lush resolutions will have shriveled. Within a month, life's thorny vines will have squeezed the last sap out of any remaining seedling that did not find good soil. You see, Jesus was not making a point that we should avoid seed-snatching Satan, worrisome weeds, and a rubble-strewn life—they're widespread. Even the best soil can become compacted or spoiled by thorns and rocks. He was urging good soil maintenance—soft hearts devoted to nurturing kingdom words to produce fruit.

Jesus was not giving His apprentices a preferential explanation so they could pass a test that the crowd would fail. Even when the disciples had a cast list and knew the storyline, their response to the parable still depended on the condition of their hearts. God is the revealer of mysteries; He will gladly show us what we need when we ask. But then His words test our hearts.

Are the ears and eyes of our hearts open? Are our hearts soft and warm to the things of God and pulsing with faith? Or are they coated with the plaque of intellectualism or religious business as usual? The mysteries of the kingdom of heaven are like seeds; humble, teachable hearts are fertile soil that will bear fruit.

Peepholes *into* God

(Context: Psalm 22:1–31.)

I will proclaim Your name to my brothers;
In the midst of the assembly I will praise You.
(Psalm 22:22. See also Hebrews 2:12.)

One rainy day during a childhood family vacation, we visited a museum that featured a doll's house. My sister was enthralled. I pretended boyish boredom. But that doll's house stamped my memory. It was gigantic. A craftsman had made it for a young girl who lived in a British stately home that is probably the setting for historical dramas now. The doll's house would fill the average living room—a palatial toy for a duchess' daughter.

Hundreds of windows spring to mind. They were two inches high by an inch wide, with dozens on each side of the five-storey house. Peering through each opening, one could see the details of a room: tiny chairs, tables, four-poster beds, pictures on the walls, little rugs, miniature cats, bowls, cups, lamps made from flashlight bulbs—everything a young (and horribly spoilt) madam would need. The windows revealed the luxurious dream world of a lavish childhood.

The names of God are like those windows—peepholes into the character and activities of God. A wall of names expresses His greatness, might, power, and supremacy; another tells of His love for humankind manifested in His desire to deliver and redeem. Several names speak of His creativity and His sustenance of His creation. Many names provide insight into His eternal nature. He is a defender and protector who reveals His wrath against ungodliness and injustice. The basement foundations of His nature are visible through His names—His holiness and righteousness and His universal position as Lord and King. But He is not a God behind high walls, with security bars blocking all access. He is the God who delights in relationships with people and allows Himself to be called the God of individuals and groups.

Jesus came and fulfilled Psalm 22. He showed us in the flesh the Character behind the names. Now we can understand the names of God as windows flung open, inviting everyone to know Him. And God's names do not open onto a lifeless dream; "names are verbal handles—handles for relationships."[1] They invite us into a relationship with a Living God.

Does your life have peepholes for people to see aspects of the nature of God?

---

1. John Avery, *The Name Quest—explore the names of God to grow in faith and get to know Him better*, (Morgan James Publishing, 2015), 9. Used with permission. This piece first appeared on *www.NamesForGod.net*.

The BLUE TOUCH PAPER

(Context: Matthew 8:1–17, 23–34; 9:1–8. Parallels: Mark 1:29–2:12; 4:35–5:20; Luke 4:38–41; 5:12–26; 7:1–10; 8:22–39.)

It was a simple job with spectacular results. I had a lot of fun that evening. The organizer had asked me to light the fuses on the fireworks for a local display. They each came with one instruction emblazoned in appropriate red or yellow: "Light the blue touch paper and stand back."

Matthew's account of Jesus' ministry immediately after the Sermon on the Mount reads like a firework display of miracles. The multitudes that had marveled at His authoritative teaching followed Him and saw the practical extent of that authority. Right there, at the foot of the mountain, *a leper came to Him, and bowed down to Him, saying, "Lord, if You are willing, You can make me clean." And He stretched out His hand and touched him, saying, "I am willing; be cleansed"* (Matthew 8:2–3).

Jesus' words acted like a flame to a short fuse. Cleansed skin spread over the leper's body like the sparks of an exploding rocket. Whoosh!

Leaving the leper to formalize his cure with a local priest, Jesus headed home to Capernaum. There, a centurion implored Him to heal his paralyzed servant. The officer understood authority. He told the great physician that he didn't need a home visit. "Just say the word." Boom! Within the hour, the servant was up again.

At Peter's house, Jesus touched the hand of His sickly hostess as though it was blue touch paper. Pow! She hopped out of bed, healthy again, eager to serve snacks.

Caught in a sudden violent storm on a boat trip across Galilee, Jesus demonstrated bold faith by rebuking the winds and waves with dramatic effect.

On the eastern shore of Galilee, Jesus and His disciples encountered violent demoniacs. A single word, "Begone!" was enough to dispatch the demons. Poooff!

Back in Capernaum, stretcher-bearers delivered a paralytic to Him. Unlike the case of the centurion's servant, Jesus mixed in a dose of forgiveness to free nerves, joints, and bones from their immobility. Fizzz!

On and on went the show. What were the fireworks for? They marked the arrival of the kingdom of heaven on earth. The boundaries of darkness retreated as Jesus toured Galilee during those days. Each miracle lit up another dark corner of the heavenly places: leprosy, for so long untouchable, was vanquished; paralysis loosened; intimidating demons driven from their territory; the untamable forces of water and air conquered. Women and despised leaders of a foreign occupying force became welcome beneficiaries of God's merciful healing. Even sin, which had dragged its victim incapacitated onto his bed, loosed its hold at Jesus' word. The kingdom of God broke through all barriers.

I hear someone saying, "But that was Jesus, the Son of God. We're different." Remember, the Spirit of the risen Jesus is given to us to live the same way as He did. For Jesus, miracles were part of everyday life. For us, the heirs of the kingdom, the challenge is to exercise our God-given kingdom authority with commands or actions whenever we see a need or an opportunity.

It's simple and fun, just like lighting the blue touch paper.

Scrumping

(Context: Genesis 1:26–3:7.)

Like every other tree in the garden, it looked nice and was good for food. Just the replenishment a person needs before and after a day tending plants and naming animals. How convenient too—right there in the middle of everything (Genesis 2:9; 3:3).

One thing was different though. God had told Adam and Eve not to eat the fruit; it was a killer (Genesis 2:17).

"But why can't I eat it? I want to try it," cried the childish voice inside.

The answer never broke the silence: "Because I said so."

The story reminds me of the day when I learned a new British slang word—scrumping.[2] A gang of my older friends decided we should sneak under a fence into a neglected orchard. Lookouts were stationed. The rest of us picked the biggest apples we could find, scoffed[3] (probably new) a few, wrapped the rest in our T-shirts, and scarpered[4] (this might be new too!).

Tempting fruit hangs at the crossroads of our lives, on the way to everywhere, at the places of decision. There is no fence. A bright strobe light and a

---

2. Check it in *The Ridiculously Comprehensive Dictionary of British Slang*, compiled by Ian Hall. It means "stealing fruit from an orchard."
3. It means, "To devour food quickly and greedily."
4. Remember this one next time you get bored using "run away."

twenty-four-hour drive-thru' make its juicy lure unavoidable. Almost invariably it looks beautiful, and the fragrance suggests sweetness, even if there is the chance of a bitter aftertaste.

The dialogue continues today. "Why can't we pick and eat?" The answer depends on perspective. What is pleasing to the eyes and good for food may well benefit flesh and bones. *The woman saw that the tree was good for food, and that it was a delight to the eyes, and that the tree was desirable to make one wise* (Genesis 3:6). "Aren't wise minds and the knowledge of good and evil worthy desires?" "It can't be sinful."

If human nature begins and ends with body and mind, then dig in. But that's not the case. We were created in the image of God, who has no form; He's Spirit. Bodies and minds must come to terms with the silent, invisible spirit in every person. That spirit waits for its own breath of life so it can live, gain strength, and become the governor of body and mind.

When our minds understand that perspective, we can make right choices. Enlightened minds discipline the body to pick fruit that feeds the spirit. Such minds have come to love the Creator; they know He is thoroughly trustworthy. If He says, "No," there's a good reason, and we don't demand explanations. The spiritual life is nourished by obedience rooted in faith and love of the Eternal Spirit.

The strength of our obedience is unknown until it is tested. That's probably why the nicest trees are planted at life's crossroads. Will we swing in quickly to feed body or mind, or will we do what the Father tells us is right? The regular passing of the test strengthens the spiritual life. It's practice at listening and obeying that trains our senses to discern good and evil—not scrumping (Heb. 5:14).

Spiritual Forensics

(Context: Acts 3:1–4:22.)

When a bomb explodes, one question every investigator wants answered is how the suspects did it. In other words, what explosive, detonator, and trigger caused the blast? And, who taught them how to assemble the device?

A spiritual bomb exploded during afternoon rush hour near the temple in Jerusalem. No one was killed or maimed. In fact, just the opposite—a lame beggar regained the strength to leap. Because the man was a feature at the temple gate, the healing caused a mass disturbance. The authorities wanted to prevent trouble spreading. The incident investigators used their best spiritual forensics to discover the power behind the troublesome healing.

Healings were not new to the Jews; the religious rulers understood that miracles happened when someone invoked a higher authority. Their question was, "Which one?" Until recent years, healing power had been scarce, the secrets guarded, and mostly used by their authorized initiates. Now a new kind of power was at work and it was beyond their control. Hence their question to Peter and John: "*By what power, or in what name, have you done this?*" (Acts 4:7)

Peter, the spokesman for the defense, was consistent in his explanation. He had said the same thing to the man and the crowd (Acts 3:6, 16).

> *Rulers and elders of the people, if we are on trial today for a benefit done to a sick man, as to how this man has been made well, let it be*

> *known to all of you and to all the people of Israel, that by the name of Jesus Christ the Nazarene, whom you crucified, whom God raised from the dead—by this name this man stands here before you in good health. He is the stone which was rejected by you, the builders, but which became the chief cornerstone. And there is salvation in no one else; for there is no other name under heaven that has been given among mankind by which we must be saved.* (Acts 4:8–12)

Many Christians believe in God's healing power. Typically, we operate with the understanding that prayer triggers healing, but Peter never recited a special prayer formula. His simple command to walk detonated the healing because it carried the authority of Jesus Christ, the Nazarene, who wills wholeness for all. In a flash, Peter and John's faith in Jesus' name must have reacted with a trace of faith in the lame man and unleashed an explosion of God's healing power (Acts 3:16).

Peter and John already knew what Paul later expressed: the name of Jesus represents the highest authority in the universe; it is the name above all names, for all time (Eph. 1:20–21; Phil. 2:9–10). Praying in Jesus' name is certainly not superficial, like using the name, "Jesus," as a magic password. Seven naïve disciples tried that—and failed in shame (Acts 19:13–17).

The disciples hid nothing from their interrogators. The inquiry was brief. It ended with a lame attempt by the authorities to prevent further "disturbances." They banned the disciples from using Jesus' name publicly. But with such a powerful name in the arsenal of their hearts, why on earth would they stop using it? Would you?

Baby Giants

(Context: 2 Samuel 21:15–22.)

When David killed Goliath in the name of God, everybody in Israel celebrated. But they forgot the facts of life—giants have babies too. Toward the end of David's reign, when David was weary from yet another Philistine uprising, the giant problem almost destroyed David. One of Goliath's big kids set out to assassinate him. The story has a moral: overcoming temptation is like overcoming giants; the roots of the problem must be dealt with.

> *Now when the Philistines were at war with Israel again, David went down, and his servants with him; and when they fought against the Philistines, David became weary. Then Ishbi-benob, who was among the descendants of the giant, the weight of whose spear was three hundred shekels of bronze in weight, had strapped on a new sword, and he intended to kill David. But Abishai the son of Zeruiah helped him and struck the Philistine and killed him. Then David's men swore to him, saying, "You shall not go out again with us to battle, so that you do not extinguish the lamp of Israel."* (2 Samuel 21:15–17)

Apparently, Goliath had four sons. When they were born, their mother and all the women of the family probably made all the usual cooing noises over them, knitted soft toys and oversized booties, and said how cute they were. From

Israel's perspective, they were sinister ogres—strong and formidable fighters. One nameless monster even had an extra finger on each hand and an extra toe on each foot (verse 20). All the better to catch you and stomp on you with.

Thankfully, David had gathered some mighty warriors around him. They stepped in when he was aged and weak and protected him from the ghastly giants. As far as we know, those four big brothers were the last giants to pester Israel. David's mighty men eliminated them like troublesome rodents.

James tells us that sin is the offspring of a chain reaction. Lust for something provides fertile ground for temptation to take root and produce sin (James 1:13–15). We often associate lust with sexual sin, but lust can refer to any intense desire. The key to overcoming many temptations is to tackle the giant called lust.

If we are alert, we will know of the birth of a giant and be able to act before it has time to grow. Unusually strong or fast-growing desires need guarding against. Monstrous cravings that expand beyond normal healthy limits should raise red flags. Never call baby giants cute! They grow surprisingly fast. Dealing with giants while they are still babies is by far the best strategy. At whatever point we become aware of them, giant desires need to be eradicated.

- Wise people gather stronger believers around them who can help them resist temptation. Accountability to others is part of overcoming temptation. Have a friend that you can call when you feel the heavy footsteps of temptation approaching. "Please pray for me."
- Remember the Scripture promise: *No temptation has overtaken you except something common to mankind; and God is faithful, so He will not allow you to be tempted beyond what you are able, but with the temptation will provide the way of escape also, so that you will be able to endure it* (1 Cor. 10:13). He's our chief warrior who defends and rescues us.
- Goliath lost his battle because David's faith in God had far more substance than Goliath's bravado. God honored David's faith and humility. When we admit our weakness and vulnerability and place our trust in God, we are in the best position to experience His deliverance.

KINGS and STARS

(Context: Matthew 2:1–12.)

Kings and stars guide all of us on our journeys with God. Kings represent human factors; stars represent the divine. We must learn to recognize the difference between them and give each factor its due weight. The magi who went to worship the newborn Christ child are an example of how it works.

Imagine them arriving in Jerusalem after their long journey. So far, they had navigated by a star that signaled a royal birth. In the city, they reverted to ordinary guidance. Kings live in capital cities, so they began inquiring there. They probably asked people who would know best: elders, leaders, military officers, priests, and government officials. Knowing the culture of Judea, they understood that this king must be the Messiah.

King Herod heard about the eccentric visitors. He bristled at talk of messiahs. Messiahs tended to rally rebels; they threatened national stability and threatened him. A quick, casual inquiry informed him that a Jewish prophet had pointed to Bethlehem as the birthplace. Sly Herod invited the magi for an audience to get an idea of the baby's age and to use the magi to locate the brat. When the magi heard Herod's invitation, it made sense to accept. Later, the magi reverted to their former method of navigation.

After hearing the king, they went their way; and behold, the star, which they had seen in the east, went on ahead of them until it came

> *to a stop over the place where the Child was to be found.*
> (Matthew 2:9)

It raises a question: why did the magi take a break from nav-star in Jerusalem? Perhaps there are two possibilities:

- Stars are not visible during the day or when skies are overcast. Could it be that the magi were so keen to find the Messiah that they could not wait for nighttime or better weather? They knew they were close, so they used their initiative and asked around.
- Bethlehem is six miles from Jerusalem. A star over Bethlehem could be mistaken for a sign over Jerusalem. It's easy to discount a tiny discrepancy in guidance. What's more, the current king in the royal palace in Jerusalem was the most likely person to have sired a royal child. Surely the magi had arrived. We can imagine their diplomatic question, "Your majesty, um . . . have you by chance had a son recently?"

Don't we take the same breaks from following God's guidance? Impatience, initiative, or assumptions take us back to human path-finding. It's not necessarily a problem. The magi made it to Bethlehem, and God upset Herod's scheme. God led them by both methods. The lesson for us is to learn the difference between kings and stars and make sure we stay focused on, and can recognize, the outcome God is leading us to.

Live Bait

(Context: John 8:1–11.)

When I want to catch rats under a house, I use smelly cheese to get their attention so that they grab it and spring the trap. The Pharisees wanted to trap Jesus. They dragged live bait, kicking and squealing perhaps, right under his nose.

> *The scribes and the Pharisees brought a woman caught in the act of adultery, and after placing her in the center of the courtyard, they said to Him, "Teacher, this woman has been caught in the very act of committing adultery. Now in the Law, Moses commanded us to stone such women; what then do You say?" Now they were saying this to test Him, so that they might have grounds for accusing Him. But Jesus stooped down and with His finger wrote on the ground. When they persisted in asking Him, He straightened up and said to them, "He who is without sin among you, let him be the first to throw a stone at her." And again He stooped down and wrote on the ground. Now when they heard this, they began leaving, one by one, beginning with the older ones, and He was left alone, and the woman where she was, in the center of the courtyard. And straightening up, Jesus said to her, "Woman, where are they? Did no one condemn you?" She said, "No one, Lord." And Jesus said, "I do not condemn you, either. Go. From now on do not sin any longer." (John 8:3–11)*

Jesus oozed with mercy, and the Pharisees knew it. Their victim had no hope of living unless Jesus intervened. She had been caught red-handed violating the seventh commandment; the penalty was clear and justified. In their eyes, Jewish religious Law prescribed the solution for sin—death by stoning would wipe the stain from among God's people. "What do you say, Jesus?" Would Jesus respect the religious system and apply it to the woman, or would He be unable to resist His insatiable appetite to extend mercy to sinners? If He reached out in mercy, the legal bar of the trap would snap down and crush Him along with that odious adulterer.

The Pharisees stood back, smirking, and watched as their rat sniffed at the trap. He scratched a little in the dust and then looked up. With a few select words, he exposed their danger.

The trap, so cleverly set for Jesus, was bigger than the Pharisees knew. If they relied on the Law to do its job, they would never escape its reach or its force. The wisest or the most guilt-conscious among the Pharisees began to blend with the crowd and shuffle away, mumbling. Soon, even the youngest, most zealous and idealistic Pharisees were gone. Only the sinner remained. Jesus had done what He so skillfully does; He had turned the trap on its makers. They were so absorbed in their religion that they refused to accept Jesus as God's solution to sin, bettering the Law. When Jesus confronted their guilt, pride propelled them back to their religious holes. Only a wretched woman had the humility to stick around to receive the guilt-free life that Jesus alone could give.

This incident shows there is no contest between law and grace in Jesus' mind; instead, the two work together. Unlike the Pharisees, Jesus knew the true role of the Law. In the absence of Jesus, the Law has the authority to throw stones at sinners; in the presence of Jesus, the Law bows to His authority. The Law exposes our sin, highlights our need for cleansing, and points to our Savior.

We have our own religious systems, don't you know? Does yours pretend to be the best solution for sin? The test of any system is whether it puts Jesus in the center and allows Him to deal with sin and dole out life. What then do *you* say?

MEET THE *the* MAGICIAN

(Context: Acts 8:5–25.)

Samaria was abuzz. Philip's proclamation of Christ had resulted in the expulsion of unclean spirits and the healing of paralytics. The power of God had set the city rejoicing. Even the esteemed magician, Simon, was baptized and became a follower of Philip. Who wouldn't want to be part of an amazing discipleship program like that? (Acts 8:5–13)

One thing was missing, though. The power of God at work through Philip had not yet come upon the new believers. So, the apostles in Jerusalem sent Peter and John to pray for an impartation of the Holy Spirit. As the apostles laid hands on members of the Samaritan church, they began receiving the Spirit. So far, so good. Many branches of the church recognize belief in Jesus, and baptism in water and the Spirit, as the first steps into the Christian life. However, Simon the magician tried to take a shortcut. He saw the effect of the Holy Spirit on people's lives, and he wanted to have the same impact. You see, Simon liked to astonish people. He loved admirers and the reputation he earned:

All the people, from small to great, were paying attention to him, saying, "This man is the Power of God that is called Great." (Acts 8:10)

However, verse 13 indicates that the miracles of God had turned the tables on Simon; the astonisher had been outdone and was himself amazed.[5] Time for a power upgrade! Simon concluded, "Never mind receiving the Spirit myself. I'll just buy a franchise and add Holy Spirit impartation to my repertoire of magic tricks." We never hear the end of Simon's story beyond Peter's stern rebuke (Acts 8:14–24). However, there's a lesson for everyone about ministering in the power of God.

Part of the preparation for serving God is to meet the magician inside each of us. We all enjoy the admiration that sometimes comes with ministry positions. No one will last long in a role if they do not bear good fruit. But our detour begins when we conclude that the success or security of our position is proportionate to what we can do or when we start to revel in a reputation. Then we start offering our prayer, worship, and Bible study times to the Lord with the secret intent of acquiring the power of God for our own glory. Nothing is a secret from God; He sees our hearts, and He does not trade power or glory.

Once we have met the magician, though, we can deal with him or her and write a better ending to our own story. The power of God is given to bring glory to Him and to set captives free. The step that Simon missed—baptism with the Holy Spirit—involves surrendering our lives to Him. The best guard against the magician mentality is to focus our lives on glorifying God, and to minister out of compassion for those who need His touch.

---

5. The same Greek word is used for "astonishing" and "amazed" in Acts 8:9 and 13.

The GREATEST FAITH

(Context: Luke 7:1–10. Parallel: Matthew 8:5–13.)

Who in the Gospel stories had the greatest faith? The disciples were late starters. Jesus commended several people for their faith but singled out one man, a non-Jewish centurion, with a remarkable observation: *"Not even in Israel have I found such great faith"* (Luke 7:9).

Was Jesus on a faith hunt? Perhaps not, but He certainly commented on it when He saw its presence or absence in people. The story of the centurion teaches us a few things about faith—and humility.

Centurions were tough men, respected by the Romans and those who accepted Roman rule. This centurion had so won the hearts of the Jewish leaders in Capernaum that it was they who came to Jesus on his behalf. "He is worthy for you to grant this to him" (Luke 7:4). The officer's beloved servant was paralyzed and in agony, about to die.[6] Jesus set out for the centurion's house.

That's when we meet humility. "I am not worthy for you to come under my roof," the officer said. He added that he considered himself unworthy of making his own request to Jesus. But don't mistake humility for an unhealthy, low self-esteem that feels disqualified to receive anything from God. The centurion's humility was in accepting his place relative to Jesus.

---

6. Luke 7:2–10 and Matthew 8:5–13 give slightly different, but not contradictory, details.

At the same time, he knew that there was no need for, and no possibility of, special qualifications to release God's favor. The centurion understood that miracles happen when the authoritative voice of God speaks them into action. He knew that the only requirement for healing was for Jesus to speak the word—that's faith. Jesus saw his humility and faith and declared, "Let it be done to you as you have believed."

Why did no Jews have that much faith? Their religion was steeped in the knowledge of God's character and power, and His faithful care for His people. Yet somehow, faith was stunted. Religion gently poisons faith. It doesn't kill it; it just weakens it. Religious knowledge breeds pride and a sense of entitlement rather than humility. Religion tangles people in lists of conditions and formulae. Religion is the human substitute for real spiritual life.

Faith keeps hearts in a posture to receive miracles from God.

The THE REVEALER *of* MYSTERIES

(Context: Daniel 2:1–49.)

I rarely lose things, except for my memory. When I forget a person's name or misplace my keys, I am grateful for the times when God answers my prayers and reminds me of a name or shows me the lost object. God longs to show us greater things. Like Daniel, we are in a relationship with God, the Revealer of Secrets[7] (Dan. 2:28–29, 47), and He wants to involve us in revealing those mysteries to others.

Daniel faced a nightmare situation. King Nebuchadnezzar had lost a night's sleep. A bad dream had left him anxious and confused. Unless someone interpreted the dream, the king would tear every advisor in Babylon limb from limb. To make matters worse, the king refused to tell anyone what the dream was. The wise men were stumped; only their gods could know, and they didn't live nearby (Dan. 2:11).

Quickly, Daniel told his three friends, and they did classic intercession. They were among the wise men of Babylon who faced destruction by the frustrated king. However, because of their relationship with the God of heaven, they could petition Him on behalf of the whole group (Dan. 2:17–18). Like them, our privileged access to the Lord is meant to benefit everyone, even people cut off from God.

---

7. Older Bibles translate the word as "mysteries".

The truly wise are humble and give glory to God (Dan. 2:27, 30). When God answered Daniel in a night vision, he immediately praised God for making the dream and its interpretation known. Daniel was granted an audience with Nebuchadnezzar. The king remarked on Daniel's insight, but Daniel pointed to the God of heaven as the Revealer of Mysteries.

> *The king said to Daniel, whose name was Belteshazzar, "Are you able to make known to me the dream which I have seen and its interpretation?" Daniel answered before the king and said, "As for the secret about which the king has inquired, neither wise men, sorcerers, soothsayer priests nor diviners are able to declare it to the king. However, there is a God in heaven who reveals secrets, and He has made known to King Nebuchadnezzar what will take place in the latter days."* (Daniel 2:26–28)

Daniel proceeded to tell the dream and give its interpretation. It concerned a statue made of four materials: gold, silver, bronze, and an odd mixture of iron and clay. A stone struck the statue and crushed it. Then the stone grew into a mountain filling the earth. Nebuchadnezzar was duly impressed. He gave Daniel lavish presents and a promotion. The king also acknowledged God as the Revealer of Mysteries.[8]

This story sets the stage for understanding biblical mysteries and our part in them.

- By definition, the mysteries of God are beyond natural human comprehension. Only God can reveal them. However, God has no interest in establishing a secret society of special initiates who learn a complex code and never share what they know. On the contrary, biblical mysteries are revealed to anyone with access to God through Jesus.
- Revealed mysteries will not sit comfortably with everyone. The gold head represented Nebuchadnezzar. The rest of the statue symbolized the

---

8. Dan. 2:47. See also Job 12:22; Dan. 2:21–22, 29.

dynasties that would follow his kingdom. Although the dream pointed beyond Nebuchadnezzar's life, the prediction about his legacy was not encouraging. The kingdoms of the world would decline and eventually be shattered and displaced by a rock-solid heavenly kingdom. Like Nebuchadnezzar, we have to bow to the truth that our lives apart from God have little and temporary significance.

- Like the dream, most biblical mysteries concern the eternal kingdom of God: its establishment by Jesus Christ, our entry into it by faith, and how it will one day envelop all human affairs. We are not excluded from the mystery of His will; rather, we are encouraged to take our place in it and find significance and a lasting legacy there.

Ask God to show you the keys to the mysteries of His kingdom, and make it your life work to share them with others.

Reflections *of a* Fisher of Men (*and* Women)

(Context: Matthew 4:18–22. Parallel: Mark 1:16–20. See also Luke 5:1–11.)

What plans we had when we were younger! We worked all hours on the lake. We saved every spare denarius, hoping to buy our next boat. What dreams! A small fleet; dominating the Galilean fishing business; building nice houses; acquiring land for animals, olive groves, and vineyards; enough servants to semi-retire. It all changed that day when Jesus walked up and said, *"Follow Me, and I will make you fishers of men"* (Matthew 4:19). Well, that's what we did.

Jesus was the first person with a plan for our lives that benefitted us as well as Him. Everyone else wanted something from us, and we wanted something from them, and no one seemed completely satisfied with the outcome. Fish traders squeezed prices down to maximize their profits; women haggled over freshness and missing fins. The tax collectors' extortions trapped us in our small business, strangling our dreams. But that's life! We will always be the ones who are the most invested in our own interests.

At first, Jesus' offer sounded as one-sided as anyone else's. Slowly we realized a difference; He offered an entirely new lifestyle that blessed both sides. You see, God is the only being in the universe that thoroughly cares about us and knows what He designed us for. He knows us better than we know ourselves. Jesus showed us how to use the Father's power to set people free from sickness, demons, and sin. It transformed them but changed us too. Serving Him in His "fishing" business, by blessing others, turned out to be more exciting and fulfilling than our wildest dreams. Mind you, it took us a few years to understand enough to make the change.

Watching Him was a big part of it. He was never selfish; He didn't need to indulge Himself because He was thoroughly satisfied in His Father. As a result, He related to people differently; He loved people without needing them. He was not bound to pamper their needs or have them meet His. He depended solely on the Father and acted like everyone should do the same. People would come to Him with selfish requests, and He would refuse. Sometimes He made His family wait. It seems that the relationships He invested in were with people, like us, who wanted to learn His ways, or with whom there was simple mutual enjoyment.

Now we try to relate in the same ways. Trusting the Father's love for us and His detailed practical care is the beginning. That helps us love others, care for them in the same way that God cares for them, and point them to Him. We don't have to meet their misguided demands. If they reject our love and care, it's not really a rejection of us. We move on and spend time helping those who take Jesus' offer seriously by doing what He says.

We thought of Him as our rabbi, or like a shepherd with his flock. But one day, after He had returned to the Father, it dawned on us—He was a fisher of people. Oh, He wasn't constantly hauling in bulging net-loads of people, but He scattered bait everywhere He went, attracting multitudes. Now we are tossing nets out to catch them. I would never have imagined such a fulfilling occupation. It blesses us to do it, but it benefits the newcomers far more when they start following Him. How ironic that we ended up in His business rather than our own.

Belief *and* Unbelief *on a* Journey

(Context: John 4:46–54.)

Fifteen miles is a long way on a tired mount, especially when belief and unbelief are wrestling inside. The royal official was riding through that transitional world between faith and sight that we all have to navigate. He had set off the previous day from Capernaum, climbing the steep trail to Cana. Jesus was there. The official had heard that He did miracles. Could He heal his son before the sickness took his life? It wasn't until he heard Jesus speak that he started to believe:

> *Jesus said to him, "Unless you people see signs and wonders, you simply will not believe." The royal official said to Him, "Sir, come down before my child dies." Jesus said to him, "Go; your son is alive." The man believed the word that Jesus spoke to him and [set off].* (John 4:48–50)

The official was plagued by doubt on his journey home. Jesus had done nothing—no wave of His hand, no medicine to rush home with. Did Jesus even glance in the direction of Capernaum? Jesus' only response was the simple statement, "Go; your son is alive." Jesus certainly didn't offer a home visit. Had the official wasted his journey? Should he have stayed home to hold his son's hand as he uttered his final words with his last breath?

But there was something authoritative about Jesus' words, especially His use of the present tense, "Your son is alive." And hadn't Jesus challenged him to believe, even without a sign? Wringing faith from Jesus' words, the royal official trotted on. As he rounded a corner and looked down the road, his heart missed a beat. Those were *his* servants hurrying up the trail. What was the news? Had his son worsened . . . or died?

> *His slaves met him, saying that his son was alive. So he inquired of them the hour when he began to get better. Then they said to him, "Yesterday at the seventh hour the fever left him." So the father knew that it was at that hour in which Jesus said to him, "Your son is alive"; and he himself believed, and his whole household.* (John 4:51–53)

Jesus' words had proved doubly true; not only had the boy recovered, but the fever had broken precisely when Jesus had made His simple declaration. The battle between belief and unbelief was won for now; important territory had been retaken from unbelief. The family, servants, and staff were so impressed by the healing that they all believed.

We face similar journeys of faith. We may have little to base our faith on—a Scripture, a previous experience, or a prophecy or prayer spoken over us. Jesus is always calling us deeper in faith. We have to clutch what we know of His character and let that fuel faith for our latest struggle. God is involved in our lives. He has the power to accomplish His will, and His will is always best for us. Let's wring faith from who God is and what He says. There is enough there to last until His words come true.

Footprints *on the* Ceiling

(Context: Colossians 3:22–25.)[9]

> *Whatever you do, do your work heartily, as for the Lord and not for people, knowing that it is from the Lord that you will receive the reward of the inheritance. It is the Lord Christ whom you serve.* (Colossians 3:23–24)

I love the bumper sticker, "My boss is a Jewish carpenter." It says so much.

I have done some mundane, dirty, and difficult jobs in my time: I have cleaned out pigsties and then spread the manure on farmland. For three months, I washed dishes in a busy restaurant. On an outreach near the Mexican border, I swept a one-acre parking lot in ninety-degree heat. However, nothing beats cleaning a dirty apartment—not even the pigsty!

When the front door almost falls off its hinges, you know you are in for trouble. The smell hits you next—a mixture of bad food, feline urine, and unwashed humans. The living room looks as though someone did oil changes right there on the carpet. The refrigerator (unplugged a week ago) buzzes with tiny fruit flies when you open the door, and a slime-induced odor slaps you like a wave. There are ways to clean up all those disasters. Ten hours later, the apartment will be habitable again. Ten hours to contemplate

---

9. This piece won an Oregon Christian Writers Cascade Award for unpublished devotionals.

how humans can live like animals—and how the heck did they get spaghetti and footprints on the ceiling?

Cleaning rental property should be on the list of dirtiest jobs—dirt that creeps under the skin into the soul. For the few months that I did it, I faced inner conflicts I had never faced before: Why should I clean up after people who live like this? Earning low wages for what is actually a skilled job is unjust. Who cares whether I get every little bit of mold out from under the window tracks? No one will notice.

That last one pointed me to the only real motivation for a job like this—Jesus cares. He cares because He is doing the same kind of deep cleaning in my own heart, with the utmost care and sacrifice.

He sees too—right into the crevices of my attitude that prefers to sweep dirt under a rug. It doesn't matter that my employer won't know I cut corners. If I leave that apartment with a smile on my face, masking frustration and self-pity, Jesus will see right through it.

But what would church folk think of their pastor scrubbing toilets and stovetops? It hardly seems like God's blessing on my life—fruitful ministry and all that. Have I done something wrong that God would reduce me to this? I mustn't tell anyone about my day job. Then I remember that Jesus was a carpenter. He probably dealt with difficult customers and felt underpaid for His skills. If Jesus could undertake menial work with dignity, then so can I. Instead of grumbling in disgust at the former occupants, I can pray for them and work as if Jesus will be the next resident.

When we labor for Jesus, doing our best never needs to be about avoiding punishment for failure; it's about the privilege of serving Him and the reward He promises.

Choose Your Blessing

(Context: Genesis 27:1–45; 35:1–15.)

Blessings come in many flavors. Jacob received two in his life. The first came as the result of trickery encouraged by a spiritually weak mother. He disguised himself in animal skins to fool his blind father, Isaac, into thinking he was blessing his eldest son, Esau, the hunter.

> *Then his father Isaac said to him, "Please come close and kiss me, my son." So he came close and kissed him; and when he smelled the smell of his garments, he blessed him and said, "See, the smell of my son is like the smell of a field which the Lord has blessed; now may God give you of the dew of heaven, and of the fatness of the earth, and an abundance of grain and new wine; may peoples serve you, and nations bow down to you; be master of your brothers, and may your mother's sons bow down to you. Cursed be those who curse you, and blessed be those who bless you." (Genesis 27:26–29)*

Like Jacob, we crave blessings like that, with their appealing flavor—a pleasing blend of prosperity and prominence, with a reassuring aftertaste of divine protection. Some of us spend our lives secretly siphoning those things from every situation and relationship we go through. We assume that it's just our nature to be takers rather than givers. We wonder why some people avoid us—it's because they hear a subtle sucking sound as we approach.

Jacob's stolen blessing turned rancid. Jacob had to pay for it by fleeing a vendetta from his brother Esau. He spent twenty years in self-imposed exile. Only when he returned to face his brother and shower gifts on him did he receive his second blessing. That came from God.

> *Then God appeared to Jacob again when he came from Paddan-Aram, and He blessed him. God said to him, "Your name is Jacob; you shall no longer be called Jacob, but Israel shall be your name."*
>
> *So He called him Israel. God also said to him, "I am God Almighty; be fruitful and multiply; a nation and a multitude of nations shall come from you, and kings shall come from you. And the land which I gave to Abraham and Isaac, I will give to you, and I will give the land to your descendants after you."* (Genesis 35:9–12)

God had renamed Jacob "Israel" at Peniel after he wrestled a heavenly messenger for a blessing before meeting Esau (Genesis 32:28). It seems that God pressed the pause button for two chapters while Israel journeyed from Peniel to Bethel. Reminding Jacob of the change of his name was like hitting PLAY again. Then God Almighty (*El Shaddai*) spelled out the details of His blessing for Israel.

What a difference there is between the blessing of man and the blessing of God. This time, God promised Israel a legacy that would extend through the generations. Like God's blessings on Abraham[10], which it echoes, it would overflow to bless other nations. It is not self-centered and short-lived; it is expansive and inclusive.

Which blessing will you and I choose for our lives? That of an immature Jacob who focused on his immediate needs and wanted his ego pampered, or that of a humbled man desperate for God's highest? Our world is so intensely focused on self-interests that our churches have absorbed some

---

10. Genesis 12:1–3; 22:15–18.

of the flavors. Yes, of course God loves to meet our needs, but should every song, sermon, and supplication focus on that?

There's a hidden blessing in store for spiritual wrestlers. Those who will step into the ring with God and refuse to let go until He blesses them will receive the reward. They are the ones who will have learned to stay in the fight of life—the fight that is required to secure a valuable spiritual legacy. At times there will be loneliness, fatigue, pain, and even dislocation. But those bitter or sour flavors will eventually give way to sweet and lasting satisfaction. Spiritual wrestlers must first allow God to meet their deepest needs and remake them as givers more than takers. Once a connection with the Source is established and the flow is in the right direction, there is no limit to the blessing that can result.

PEOPLE *of* LYSTRA

(Context: Acts 14:6–22.)

People of Lystra, *"Why are you doing these things? We are also men of the same nature as you, and preach the gospel to you in order that you should turn from these vain things to a living God, who made the heaven and the earth and the sea, and all that is in them."* (Acts 14:15)

Paul and Barnabus were responding to a Lystran crowd about to sacrifice oxen to them and decorate them with garlands as gods. It was all because Paul had spotted a faith-filled lame man and had healed him. The crowd had concluded that Barnabus and Paul must be Zeus and his son Hermes, respectively. The people were mistaken. As soon as a translator explained, Paul was quick to correct them. But before he could express himself fully and share about Jesus, a religious lynch mob caught up with him and knocked him unconscious.

The incident challenges us to examine ourselves for mistaken ideas. Do we draw wrong conclusions about God's interactions with us? Here's how Paul might have continued:

"People of Lystra, you are mistaken. The miracle you saw is certainly out of this world, but it's not from the gods you worship. And it comes for a different purpose than you suppose. You see, we did not heal the man. We are not gods; we are not even outstanding people. But God uses us to show

His compassion to the needy and to glorify His name. Miracles don't shine a spotlight on the person who does them; they highlight God.

"People of Lystra, look how powerful the true God is. But notice how He cares for individuals. Don't think that He is aloof and angry. He is not grumpy and grumbling in a distant heaven. He does not need appeasing with special rituals. Don't cower from him in anxiety or shame. Go closer. Get to know Him.

"People of Lystra, don't misread manifestations of God. His signs don't mean that your imagined gods are real. They are not signs that your gods have come down to bless your lusts and indulgences. Miracles are not the endorsement of your philosophies or the activation of your dreams. They are not a pat on your back to send you skipping on your own chosen way. No, the signs point to a new way—God's way.

"People of Lystra, miracles are like the first fruit on a tree. They give a taste of the way of Jesus, the true man-God. They show it leads somewhere sweet. Your way is pointless, fruitless ('vain' is the word I used before). Did you ever truly benefit from worshiping your gods? Leave your aimless ways. Ditch your gods. Turn to the new way."

People of ___.

The
HILL COUNTRY

(Context: Numbers 13:1–14:45.)

When Moses dispatched twelve spies to the hill country of Canaan, he gave them a checklist for their observations:

    Are the people strong/weak?
    Are they few/many?
    Is the land good/bad?
    Are the dwellings in camps/fortresses?
    Do you see many trees?

"And while you are there, bring back some fruit." (Numbers 13:17–20)

The spies returned with their completed intelligence report and a super-sized cluster of grapes.

> *We came in to the land where you sent us; and it certainly does flow with milk and honey, and this is its fruit. Nevertheless, the people who live in the land are strong, and the cities are fortified and very large; and indeed, we saw the descendants of Anak there.*
>
>   *Then Caleb quieted the people before Moses and said, "We should by all means go up and take possession of it, for we will certainly prevail over it." But the men who had gone up with him said, "We are not*

able to go up against the people, because they are too strong for us."
(Numbers 13:27–28, 30–31)

Our Christian lives are a series of faith challenges. Each one presents a question, just as the hill country of Canaan did. We can never see past the ridge hiding the future; we always face the question, what lies beyond it? Is it good or bad? Are the obstacles easy to overcome or guarded by indomitable giants?

At each challenge, we gather three sets of information:

- Tangible facts
- Our perception or interpretation of those facts
- God's word about the situation

The facts and our interpretations comprise what we call common sense. Ten spies and a fearful nation listened to common sense and refused to fight. "They are too strong for us." Only Joshua and Caleb considered the information from God's perspective.

> *They spoke to all the congregation of the sons of Israel, saying, "The land which we passed through to spy out is an exceedingly good land. If the Lord is pleased with us, then He will bring us into this land and give it to us—a land which flows with milk and honey. Only do not rebel against the Lord; and do not fear the people of the land, for they will be our prey. Their protection is gone from them, and the Lord is with us; do not fear them."* (Numbers 14:7–9)

Joshua and Caleb saw past the intimidating intelligence to vital spiritual truths. Canaan was God's promised land for Israel. God was with them, and so the Canaanites were as good as beaten. He had already removed the protection of Canaan; the land was up for grabs. Common sense has its place, but spiritual sense emboldens us to accomplish God's purposes.

Your mission, should you choose to accept it, is to apply God's word to the circumstances you face and respond to them in faith.

Pssst... Wanna See an Angel?

(Context: Matthew 4:1–11; Luke 22:39–46.
Parallels: Matthew 26:36–46; Mark 14:32–42; Luke 4:1–13.)

Now, before you misunderstand me, let me make it absolutely clear that chasing angels is a bad idea. Angels do not want our worship. They are spiritual beings serving to glorify God; they point us to Him. So let's keep our focus on Him. However, there are two incidents worth considering.

In the Gospels, angels proclaim the birth of Jesus and explain to Joseph and Mary what is happening. They appear at the empty tomb and after Jesus' ascension. Jesus said they would accompany the Son of Man when He returns, and gather in the harvest. But twice we are told they ministered to Jesus. That's interesting.

Matthew and Mark tell us that angels ministered to Jesus when the devil gave up tempting Jesus: "Then the devil left Him; and behold, angels came and began to serve Him" (Matthew 4:11, see also Mark 1:12–13). Luke comments, "When the devil had finished every temptation, he left Him until an opportune time" (Luke 4:13).

Maybe that opportune time arrived in Gethsemane. It was perhaps Jesus' most vulnerable moment. He knew what was about to happen—the betrayal, abandonment, false accusations, verbal and physical abuse, and one of the most shameful and agonizing deaths ever invented. Luke says Jesus was in such agony that His sweat glands oozed blood that dripped to the ground (Luke 22:44). How tempting it must have been to call the entire thing off, to summon twelve angelic legions to prevent His arrest (Matthew 26:53). But He resisted.

> *"Father, if You are willing, remove this cup from Me; yet not My will, but Yours be done." Now an angel from heaven appeared to Him, strengthening Him.* (Luke 22:42–43)

In both incidents, Jesus' refusal to use His position and power to serve or preserve His own life released God's help. For us, that help might be a wave of God's presence, the Spirit of God lifting our spirits. Sometimes we identify it as His grace or favor. Why did God send angels on these two occasions? Most angel behavior fits a simple pattern: they deliver God's messages and activate His will. In these two instances, the angels ministered strength. Perhaps angels were the most magnificently tangible and unmistakable way to support Jesus in His choice to do the Father's will.

The take-home lesson is that God supports us when we make right choices, no matter what they cost us. He is searching for hearts that are fully devoted to Him (2 Chronicles 16:9). Whenever we resist temptation and do God's will for His glory, we can be sure of His grace, favor, joy, blessing, fruit, breakthrough, spiritual anointing, or whatever kind of strength and encouragement He might send. It's tough and lonely facing testing times. Perhaps there will seem to be little help in the midst of them, but once we surrender ourselves to God, His refreshment comes. It won't matter whether it's an angel or not—it's from Him.

BETRAYAL

(Parallels: Matthew 26:47–56; Mark 14:43–50; Luke 22:47–53; John 18:1–11.)

It was one of those weeks. First, a customer became awkward about paying his overdue bill. Then something appropriate that I had said in private was repeated to a third party. By the time I heard about it, it was completely distorted and made me sound bad—like the product of a game of Chinese Whispers. Then, at the end of the week, I experienced betrayal by a friend who had misunderstood me and interpreted my words as critical.

I felt beaten up, trodden down, torn apart, and pierced to the core. Instead of being my usual buoyant self, I wanted to slide into a hole and sleep for a long time until the storm of accusations passed. Why on earth would God allow all this? I could handle the unpleasant customer, but the Christian friends! Surely God was as upset as I was.

It was then that I realized His plan. He wanted to expose my reactions to the betrayal and misunderstandings. I had withdrawn. "Don't smile at me; I have no smiles left to return." I had run a hot bathtub of self-pity, filled it with soothing bubbles, and slid as far into it as I could—to wallow. I had no care or energy left for other people, especially if they needed something.

What a contrast to Jesus. While Judas' betraying kiss still glistened, wet on Jesus' cheek, Jesus stepped in as peacemaker and healer. He healed a servant's severed ear after Peter had sliced it off. He stopped the foolish swordplay of the disciples and prevented a small massacre. He knew He could summon an angel army instantly, but He chose to allow the Scriptures to be fulfilled.

That contrast highlights the difference between my fleshly reaction to life and the response of the Holy Spirit. Pierce my human side and you will see retaliation or retreat. Betray, mock, flog, or crucify Jesus and nothing but the fruit and power of the Spirit flow out. He never missed a beat. Spirit love, power, and truth kept coming.

> *For God has not given us a spirit of timidity, but of power and love and discipline. Therefore do not be ashamed of the testimony of our Lord or of me His prisoner, but join with me* in suffering for the gospel according to the power of God. (2 Timothy 1:7–8)

Realizing God's plan comforted me. If betrayal and false accusations are His way of getting me to make more room for the Holy Spirit, then I accept. How about you?

The HALL *of* FAITH

(Context: Hebrews 11:1–19.)

The sign that greets us as we enter the Hebrews "hall of faith" provides a definition of faith:

> *Now faith is the certainty of things hoped for, a proof of things not seen. For by it the people of old gained approval.* (Hebrews 11:1–2)

Wandering through the hall, we get a few details about seventeen hard-hitting faith players. Seven more are mentioned by name. Nineteen times the chapter uses the phrase, "by faith ——," to tell of their exploits. The descriptions follow a pattern that fits the definition we saw at the door. What unseen object was the person longing for? Most of all, how did they turn faith in their unseen object of hope into action? Let's look more at the list of actions and objects—what is included and (perhaps more interesting) what is not included. Abraham is typical of the pattern:

> *By faith Abraham, when he was called, obeyed by going out to a place which he was to receive for an inheritance; and he left, not knowing where he was going. By faith he lived as a stranger in the land of promise, as in a foreign land, living in tents with Isaac and Jacob, fellow heirs of the same promise; for he was looking for the*

> *city which has foundations, whose architect and builder is God.*
> (Hebrews 11:8–10)

Abraham is a double star; he is noted for doing two related things "by faith." His first "action" was to leave the family home in Haran and cross a desert to an unknown destination. The second action involved a semi-nomadic life. As with every other member of the hall of faith, Abraham's actions involved personal cost or risk.

Turning to the object of Abraham's faith, the passage tells us he had his eyes set on the city of God. Surveying the list of faith objects in the chapter confirms that Abraham's fitted the pattern. First, God revealed it; a wishful-thinking human did not make it up. In addition, it had more to do with fulfillment of the promise to the nation, not just to an individual and his clan, and it often extended beyond the horizon of death. Abraham was so motivated by a desire for God to dwell with men, and believed in it so much, that He spent a lifetime camping. Imagine!

Among the grand objects of faith and the corresponding sacrificial actions in Hebrews 11, I see none of the everyday items that are the bulk of the buzz at many church meetings. It might be worth taking a few minutes to list your objects of faith in a column and write your actions next to them. When I analyze my faith objects, I come up with the following list:

- Health for a friend
- Provision
- Resolution of problems at work
- Good weather for our next vacation
- A School of Ministry for my church

Quite a variety! I'm challenged because it's easy to become absorbed in self-centered and short-term visions, hardly any of which were initiated by God. They mostly benefit me and involve little or no risk or personal investment. Often my "actions" amount to prayer and a small financial contribution. Some are, frankly, trivial. For those items, I'm not expecting even a mention in heaven's hall of faith!

Now, God's not short of blessings; He's happy to lavish us with personalized extras. But perhaps part of maturing in the Lord is to extend our lists to include more items with roots in God's eternal purposes. At the same time, presumably our conviction that such objects of faith are worth a wholehearted commitment will grow stronger.

Invite God to reveal new objects of faith to you and to call you to new levels of action. See where it leads!

A Resignation Speech

(Context: 1 Kings 19:1–18.)

Do your times with the Lord end just as they begin or do you change?

God's question to Elijah at Horeb, the mountain of God, is a question for all of us as we approach God in our devotions or church meetings. "What are you doing here?" Elijah seemed to have no other objective than to run as far from trouble as he could and deliver a resignation speech to God. He was done. That's sad; there are higher reasons to pursue God's presence.

It is strange how even success can fail to invigorate us. Elijah had just come from Mount Carmel and a showdown with four hundred and fifty pagan prophets. Ba'al had ignored their invocations; God had answered Elijah with fire. Then Elijah had slaughtered the prophets of Ba'al. Jezebel was livid. She swore to destroy Elijah. Even his victory on Carmel did not instill enough confidence in Elijah for him to persevere against her threats.

So, Elijah ran a day past the southern border. He slumped under a tree and groaned, "It is enough; now, O Lord, take my life, for I am not better than my fathers" (1 Kings 19:4). Presumably Elijah expected God to take him in his sleep—much better than the slow, painful death that vicious Jezebel had in mind for him. Strengthened by an angel, Elijah went forty more days to a cave on Mount Horeb, where God asked His question.

> *"What are you doing here, Elijah?"*
> *And he said, "I have been very zealous for the Lord, the God of armies; for the sons of Israel have abandoned Your covenant, torn down Your altars and killed Your prophets with the sword. And I alone am left; and they have sought to take my life."* (1 Kings 19:9–10)

Powerful earthquake, wind, and fire blasted the mountain. The rocks shattered at the force. But it was a gentle silence that got Elijah's attention so that he moved to the cave entrance. The Lord's voice repeated the question. Elijah gave exactly the same answer. In essence: "Despite my zeal, I feel I am still losing the battle."

What other answer could there be? Elijah faced fearsome opposition. He felt intense loneliness (though he did rather exaggerate his isolation[11]). He was exhausted. Nothing seemed different. Elijah saw only one exit—resignation.

But didn't Elijah miss a note of invitation in God's question? "What do you *want* to happen here?" Our times with God have many possibilities. Do we use them to vent, demand, argue, beg, or to struggle as though we might then qualify for something? Or do we bask in potent, God-filled silence? In the presence of God, things change. Earthquakes, wind, and fire have the power to rearrange rocks; the gentle voice of God has the power to rearrange perceptions and situations. That's why true worship is so doubly powerful. True worship is surrender. It gives God permission to change whatever He wants—situations and ourselves. In worship, we focus on the glory and sovereignty of God, not on our circumstances or our inability to deal with them.

I wonder how Elijah's story could have ended. If he had spent time in praise and thanks for that amazing demonstration of God's power on Mount

---

11. 1 Kings 18:4, 13; 19:18.

Carmel and the elimination of hundreds of pagan prophets, perhaps he would have had the strength to face Jezebel. Perhaps he would have ended her evil influence over King Ahab and Israel. I wonder how our lives would progress if we made a wise decision now about what we will do with our victories and what we will seek in the presence of God from here on.

The MULTIVITAMIN GOS-PILL

Multivitamins are useless if they remain in the container. We must swallow them. Would anyone be so foolish as to buy a jar and leave it unopened on the kitchen counter? Yet perhaps we do that with the gospel. You see, the *idea* of "the gospel" is like the unopened pot. Sometimes we think that buying into the gospel by becoming Christians is enough. However, if we don't absorb it into our everyday lives, it is about as wasted as the multivits on the top shelf.

"Gospel" is one of those Christian words that everyone thinks they are expected to understand and supposed to explain to others, but many are too embarrassed to admit that they are not sure they have it all straight. Mention it in a gathering of Christians and I bet there are at least a few who nod and smile but are glad you don't put them on the spot by asking for an explanation. So, for everyone's sake, let's look at what the biblical gospel container says about the gospel. Like a multivitamin pill, it has many aspects, all vital to real life.

Most vitamins are concentrated in various plant or animal products. Often the New Testament speaks of the gospel (or better, good news) in terms of God or Jesus. It is the gospel of God or His Son, Jesus Christ (Mark 1:1, 14). In a sense, the origin of the good news is God Himself, through His Son, Jesus. Jesus' death on the cross is the source of every ingredient of the good news. In another sense, the good news is concentrated in Jesus. We need Him in our lives.

But what is it about Jesus that is so good? The Bible lists several ingredients found in Him and in what He did.

- Matthew makes a big deal about the kingdom of God. *"Jesus was going about in all of Galilee, teaching in their synagogues and proclaiming the gospel of the kingdom, and healing every disease and every sickness"* (Matt. 4:23; 9:35). Kings rule over kingdoms. The good news that Jesus proclaimed and demonstrated was that our King is wonderfully good, and His power is unsurpassed. What's more, He cares so much about human problems that He uses that power to make a difference right where we live.
- The Christmas angel announced good news of *"a Savior, who is Christ the Lord"* (Luke 2:11). It is good news about salvation (Eph. 1:13). Jesus saved us from an oppressive tyrant called Satan. He set us free from slavery to sin. And because sin results in death, we have been spared from spiritual death.
- Another facet of salvation is peace (Rom. 10:15; Eph. 6:15). The biblical idea of peace is well-being or wholeness in every area of life.
- Paul called it *"the gospel of God's grace"* (Acts 20:24).[12] Grace means favor. God did us a favor by providing Jesus as a sacrifice to pay the penalty for our sin and restore our relationship with Him as Father and King. He adopted us into His family.
- It is *"the gospel of the glory of Christ"* (2 Cor. 4:4–6). Jesus showed us what the glory of God looks like when it is condensed into a human life. That's certainly nice news, but the really great news is that we are now destined to share that glory (2 Thess. 2:13–14; 2 Tim. 2:8–10). It begins today—if we take the pills.

---

12. In the next verse, Paul linked it to the kingdom.

Directions (adults and children)

Jesus made it clear that good news only gets out of the container and into our lives when we "repent and believe in" it (Mark 1:15). Repenting means rethinking life and then changing our behavior. When we believe (or have faith in) something or someone, our trust is so great that we invest everything.

One pill is not enough. To experience the greatest benefits of life as a reconciled child of the King we must continue to ingest the good news. That means we repeatedly choose to trust Him so much that we do what He says, even when His way is not as tasty as the alternatives (2 Thess. 2:15).

Warning

Side-effects may include but are not limited to: what unbelievers call "rash" decisions to do what God says out of love and faith, irritation of family and friends, spiritual growth spurts, excitement, occasional anxiety, peace that passes all understanding, and everlasting longevity.

Become a Distributor

No special qualifications are required to promote the good news. Don't worry if you can't remember all the ingredients. What Jesus did in your life is good news worth sharing. Start there. And, when God shows you a wound or a deficiency in someone, that's an opportunity to offer a sample from the pot.

Rhema *or* Rabbit Trail?

(Context: Luke 5:1–11.)

I often get weary doing things that seem fruitless or mundane. I fear that promising paths will turn into impassable rabbit trails. There seems to be no point in getting exhausted if there will be no return on my investment. Simon and his partners felt something like that one morning after catching no fish all night. They were cleaning nets and probably getting ready to slouch home and take a long nap.

> *[Jesus] saw two boats lying at the edge of the lake; but the fishermen had gotten out of them and were washing their nets. And He got into one of the boats, which was Simon's, and asked him to put out a little distance from the land. And He sat down and continued* teaching the *crowds from the boat. Now when He had finished speaking, He said to Simon, "Put out into the deep water and let down your nets for a catch." Simon responded and said, "Master, we worked hard all night and caught nothing, but I will do as You say* [rhema] *and let down the nets." (Luke 5:2–5)*

Simon already knew enough about Jesus to take Him seriously. When Jesus spoke, things happened. So, because Jesus said it, the fishermen launched back into the lake and dropped the nets again. The result was completely different, just as Jesus had said.

I want to follow Simon's example and be willing to do what Jesus says, even if my past disappointments suggest it might be pointless. Our willingness to obey rests on our love for the Lord and our trust in Him. Our experience of Him (or the stories we know about Him) assures us that His direction is guaranteed and accurate. Experience reinforces faith in His bidding. But an act of faith always starts with a word from God.

The "as You say[13]" that Simon referred to translates *rhema* (which is "a word"). The way the Greek word is used in the Bible fits a rough pattern; it often refers to specific directional statements, prophecies, promises, or divine announcements. It is used of inspired and deliberate statements that come true. The association with fulfillment is so strong that the word often refers to the results themselves. *Rhema* frequently occurs in the stories of the birth of Jesus.

As we follow Jesus, He teaches us to discern the difference between His *rhema* voice and distracting voices. When we do what He shows us, it bears fruit. But that raises another doubt that many of us struggle with. Will He speak to me, and, if He does, will I be able to hear Him? Unless we are certain of promises like: "My sheep hear my voice" and "He will guide you into all the truth,"[14] we will tend to listen with little expectation. No one waits for His voice unless they expect Him to speak. Some of us find it more comforting to devise a plan of our own just to feel like we are doing something productive. Others prefer to put the nets away and spend the day in a recliner.

Specific *rhema* words from the Lord are an important part of His guidance. So let's listen.

---

13. Older translations often have "at Your bidding."
14. John 10:27; 16:13.

A Sigh at Sunrise

(Context: Psalm 130:1–8.)

Psalm 130 begins with an anguished cry for the Lord to meet some deep request; it ends with unswerving hope. Sin might separate us from God for a while, but repentance breaks the power of iniquity[15] (or guilty deeds) and restores us to God. God forgives His people because of His loving commitment to them.[16] Even if iniquity does divert people from God, they can be sure that "He will redeem Israel from all his guilty deeds" (Psalm 130:8). Nothing stops the Lord from answering those who cry out to Him sincerely. That assurance leads to the picture of watchmen, sandwiched in the middle of the psalm.

> *I wait for the Lord, my soul waits,*
> *and I wait for His word.*
> *My soul waits in hope for the Lord*
> *more than the watchmen for the morning;*
> *yes, more than the watchmen for the morning.* (Psalm 130:5–6)

---

15. Straying from or twisting the abundant life that God prescribes for His people.
16. "Lovingkindness" (NASB) or "unfailing love" (NIV) are common translations of the Hebrew word in verse 7.

What did morning mean to watchmen? Watchmen were posted on the walls of a city to warn of attacks. Invaders preferred the cover of dark to launch surprise raids. While the city slept, the watchmen bore heavy responsibility for everyone's safety. A sleeping sentry might face the death penalty.

Watchmen spent the night battling eye strain, fatigue, fear, cold, loneliness, and boredom. Morning promised warmth. The sun illuminates everything, bringing relief to the eyes and restoring color and texture to a dull, flat world. As dawn began to break, the watchmen could sigh with relief that attacks were now unlikely. The sunrise meant breakfast, a chance to sleep, and laughter with family and friends.

We experience the spiritual equivalent of a sigh at sunrise when the Lord breaks through for us after a long wait. An answered prayer; the restoration of His presence; His reassuring voice—all evoke relief in our hearts. If we don't get complete answers, at least we gain perspective on what He is doing. Watchmen never doubt that dawn will come. Every sunrise is unique, but the sun never fails. We can wait on the Lord with even greater assurance that He will come through in His time. "His going forth is as certain as the dawn" (Hosea 6:3). There is no place for hopelessness or doubt. Turn any impatience into expectancy. He will answer.

In light of that assurance, times of waiting in the dark should be exciting. He is preparing us for a breakthrough. God is about to birth a new day in our lives.

The GRAND THEMES *of* JESUS

Spectacular dances performed at epic events like opening ceremonies for the Olympic Games are arranged around grand themes. Directors and choreographers weave the steps, music, costumes, backdrop, lighting, and props to maximum effect. Audiences gasp and cheer when they see everything syncing perfectly and the themes popping.

Jesus' life was a dance. Centuries of prophetic announcements formed the backdrop. Props were provided by the human spectrum surrounding Him with their aches and anxieties, doubts and demons, wickedness and weaknesses, pettiness and prejudices, fears and failures, hype, hypocrisy, and occasional humility. The grand themes? Well, if you had to summarize what Jesus accomplished on earth, what would you say they were?

- Many people immediately say that He died to redeem us from sin to restore our relationship with God. That's true, of course. But let's not forget four other broad accomplishments or themes of His dance.
- Jesus revealed the Father (John 14:8–9). The prophets had said a few things about the nature of God as a Father. However, fathers are only really known as fathers from how they and their children interact. Only Jesus, the Son of God, could reveal a heavenly Father with a heartbeat.

- From Jesus' first proclamation to His last instructions, with many demonstrations and explanations in between, He was all about the kingdom of God (Mark 1:15; Acts 1:3).
- He was faithful to make disciples who continued His work and made more disciples (John 17:6–19).
- John the Baptist said Jesus would send the Holy Spirit (John 1:33). Jesus returned to the Father to do just that so His followers would have direction and power (John 16:7; 20:22; Acts 1:8).

Why is it important to understand all the grand themes in Jesus' dance? Because we are called to follow Him and to become like Him. His dance is our dance . . . in part. The first and last items He already completed. No one ever needs to repeat Jesus' sacrifice, and the Spirit is already poured out. However, we should tell others about Jesus, explain what He did for us, share about our interactions with the Father, extend His kingdom, and make more disciple-making disciples who live in the direction and power of His Spirit.

God continues to dance the last four of His themes. When we learn the steps of those themes, we will be in sync with God. Then we can expect the greatest blessing and fruit in what we do. Anything else might be a waste of time. So, when we reflect on our lives, do the grand themes pop?

But a caution about learning: Many of us get caught up in classes and study. However, learning takes time, and we will only ever learn a fraction of God's ways.[17] Our relationships with God begin at the instant of adoption. A child that dances cares little about skill or understanding; its joy is in dancing with its father. Although we will never know exactly what God is doing, being with Him as He does it is enough. Following His lead is where the fun and fruit of dancing with God lie.

---

17. Someone said it takes 10,000 hours to become an expert in anything. That's five years of forty-hour weeks, enough to gain a bachelor's and a master's degree.

Earthquake Pre-prayer-edness

(Context: Acts 16:11–40.)

It's strange how we can read a passage repeatedly and miss a basic point. That happened to me with the story of Paul and Silas in prison for preaching the gospel when an earthquake struck.

> *About midnight, Paul and Silas were praying and singing hymns of praise to God, and the prisoners were listening to them; and suddenly there was a great earthquake, so that the foundations of the prison were shaken; and immediately all the doors were opened and everyone's chains were unfastened. When the jailer awoke and saw the prison doors opened, he drew his sword and was about to kill himself, thinking that the prisoners had escaped. But Paul called out with a loud voice, saying, "Do not harm yourself, for we are all here!"* (Acts 16:25–28)

If I was in prison and the doors came unhinged, I would bolt for the nearest bus to freedom. At first glance, Paul and Silas seem crazy to sit in jail with the door open. Were they crazy, or did they display a delightful dignity that we are supposed to have too?

The key is in verse 25. Prayer and worship were so habitual for Paul and Silas that chains and bruises did not deter them. I might have been praying for an earthquake or an angel to miraculously free me; that was not their prayer. Somehow their prayers and praises readied them to ignore the flight instinct and participate in a kingdom agenda. They had a different way of looking at life.

Notice the three things Paul and Silas accomplished after the jailer arrived (Acts 16:29–40). First, they led him and his household to faith in Jesus. Then they confronted the magistrates who had abused their position by beating and imprisoning Paul and Silas without trial. Finally, they encouraged Lydia's house church.

Paul and Silas' prayers and worship had prepared them so that, when the earthquake came, they followed God's agenda. You see, their natural instincts had become kingdom ones. While the dust settled, both men instinctively stayed put. As opportunities unfolded, they acted as God's agents with faith and dignity. They explained salvation to a terrified jailer, restored a little of God's justice to the city, and helped equip a fledgling church to spread the kingdom further in Philippi. God wants us to be so attuned to Him that we view open doors through His eyes, even if we don't understand the details of His plans.

Now, some of us feel we are in some kind of prison that keeps us from serving God to the full. Approaching God in prayer and worship will transform us and align us with God's ways. If you want to know the will of God, ask to have the mind of God. We will see through those walls that pretend to confine our lives. We will realize that being trapped is only temporary—bolts and bars are no obstacle for God. We'll gain a deep confidence that every heavenly resource is at hand for us to accomplish His purposes once the doors open.

Freedom often provides opportunities for self-indulgence. Only when we are single-minded about the will of God will we be able to ignore inappropriate pursuits and fleeting feelings. Then we will be responsible with our freedom, using it as a platform for kingdom business.

It is during waiting periods and times of blockage that God prepares us on the inside for life on the outside.

MAN
in the SPOTLIGHT

(Context: Matthew 21:1–11. Parallels: Mark 11:1–10; Luke 19:29–38; John 12:12–15.)

Once in a while, God reveals something to us that has all the signs of divine involvement but seems to make little sense at that moment. Palm Sunday must have been like that for the disciples.

Jesus' triumphal entry into Jerusalem served one purpose. It fulfilled predictive prophecy, but in a way that no one grasped at the time. The crowd understood Jesus as a prophet but missed His full significance. The disciples were puzzled.

> *These things His disciples did not understand at the first; but when Jesus was glorified, then they remembered that these things were written of Him, and that they had done these things for Him.* (John 12:16)

Predictive prophecies are like recessed spotlights in an artist's studio. The lights themselves are incidental, and they should be inconspicuous. The studio designer intended them to shine on an object so that it would be easily recognized and clear. When a display stand is empty, spotlights have no subject to illuminate, so the beams fall on odd places like the wall or the floor. If we look directly at the lights, they dazzle and confuse us. As Jesus stepped onto the stage of history, the purpose of the diverse prophetic beams became evident. They shone on Him.

Matthew understood the significance later. When he wrote his Gospel, he pointed out two prophetic beams converging on Jesus as He rode into Jerusalem just before His crucifixion.

> *Say to the daughter of Zion, "Behold your King is coming to you, gentle, and mounted on a donkey, even on a colt, the foal of a beast of burden."* (Matthew 21:5)

Isaiah had proclaimed, "Say to the daughter of Zion, 'Lo, your salvation comes; Behold His reward is with Him, and His recompense before Him'" (Isa. 62:11). Zechariah had said, "Rejoice greatly, O daughter of Zion! Shout in triumph, O daughter of Jerusalem! Behold, your king is coming to you; He is just and endowed with salvation, humble and mounted on a donkey, even on a colt, the foal of a donkey" (Zech. 9:9). The two prophets' spotlights converged on Jesus as He entered Jerusalem. In Yeshua' (Yahweh is salvation), salvation was embodied and ready to do a work surpassing all previous works.[18]

Two take-home lessons:

- Sometimes God needs only one purpose to do something. On Palm Sunday, He was delighted to turn the attention of six hundred years of prophetic history on Jesus and glorify Him as the Savior King.
- Like Matthew, we should carefully note any puzzling words that God speaks to us. It sometimes takes years for words and circumstances to converge and make sense. When they do, we're ready to embrace His purposes.

---

18. Adapted from a chapter on the salvation names of God in John Avery, *The Name Quest: Explore the names of God to grow in faith and get to know Him better*, (Morgan James Publishing, 2015), 300–301. Used with permission.

Kites without Strings

The Kite Festival in Lincoln City on the Oregon coast is worth visiting. Hundreds of multi-colored kites in a fascinating range of designs swoop and swirl between blue sky and golden sand. The simple ones tug on a single string. Skilled flyers maneuver the larger and more complex models using two or more strong lines. The string might seem to tether the kite to its earthbound owner. In fact, it holds the kite in the wind at the right angle to soar. Tugging it, the owner gently tilts the kite to make it twist and dive in the breeze. If a string snaps, the kite will float on the wind for a while, but eventually, it will lose its aerodynamics and flutter to the ground.

Christians are like kites.

> *Beloved, this is now the second letter I am writing to you in which I am stirring up your sincere mind by way of a reminder, to remember the words spoken beforehand by the holy prophets and the commandment of the Lord and Savior spoken* by your apostles. (2 Peter 3:1–2)

We live in an age when more and more people are detaching their Christianity from Scripture. Personal opinions often carry more weight than Scripture. Yet the Bible remains our only legitimate and objective standard of spiritual truth. Consider Peter's breakdown of the two parts of the Bible: God's primary purpose for the Old Testament was to point us to Jesus; the New Testament is based on eyewitness accounts of Jesus' life, death, and resurrection, and points out the implications of those historical events for the Christian life. Much of the Old Testament was penned by or about prophets like Moses, Samuel, Isaiah, Jeremiah, and many others. Most of the apostles were men who had been with Jesus from His baptism until His ascension. Jesus' ministry and His miraculous resurrection electrified them. It compelled them to speak and write about Jesus, regardless of any personal cost to them. Our New Testament is the result. The Bible is the message about Jesus and our new life with Him.

Peter knew the importance of the message for the Christian life. So, he urged us to remember the words that now form our Bible. What then do those prophets say? And what are the commandments of Jesus? In the original languages, the Bible contains about half a million words.[19] Can and should we condense them into a few favorite passages?

I suggest that we must approach Scripture in two ways. First, make a habit of reading portions of the Bible every day. Have a plan so that you eventually read through the entire Bible. One year is manageable for many people.[20] Take longer if you need to. Second, ask Him for specific passages relevant to your current situation. God speaks to us in the details of His word, but He also communicates through the messages that span entire books or sections of the Bible.

Occasionally I hear people grumble about the Bible as though it is boring, out of date, and somehow restricts the refreshing breeze of the Holy Spirit. I'm excited to see the Spirit move too, but the Spirit will never do or say anything that is not consistent with Scripture. The word of God is like the string of a kite. Through it, the Lord can direct His people. The Bible anchors us in the current of God's purposes. Floating in the wind with no connection to God's word might feel like freedom, but it's doomed to end. Christian

---

19. Hebrew and Greek are more concise and expressive languages than English. Our versions run to about three-quarters of a million words.
20. It requires reading about three chapters each day.

kites without strings sail jubilantly into the heavens, only to exit the spiritual wind. In the doldrums, they sag and flop to earth in a confused heap, wondering what it was all about. The wind of the Spirit is certainly blowing and is touching many lives with the love, truth, and power of God. But it never blows believers beyond the reach of the Bible. Christian kites held in the wind of the Spirit by the living word of God are a spectacular display of the life that God intends for His people.

About the Author

John Avery is the author of *The Name Quest: Explore the Names of God to Grow in Faith and Get to Know Him Better* (Morgan James Publishing, 2015). *The Name Quest* won the 2016 Oregon Christian Writers' Cascade Award for nonfiction. His most recent compilations of short pieces, *The Questions of Jesus*, and *The Kingdom of God* were published in 2022 and 2023, respectively.

John is a trained teacher with over thirty years' experience as a Bible teaching pastor, small group leader, missionary, and disciple maker. He has lived in England, Israel, Africa, and the Caribbean, ministering with Youth With A Mission (YWAM), international student ministry, and local churches. He and his wife, Janet, now make their home in Oregon. John likes to hike, snowshoe, and cross-country ski. John writes short, thought-provoking Bible devotionals at *www.BibleMaturity.com* many of which will be compiled into books like this one. He maintains a comprehensive resource for all the names of God at *www.NamesForGod.net*.

Additional Resources

The QUESTIONS of JESUS

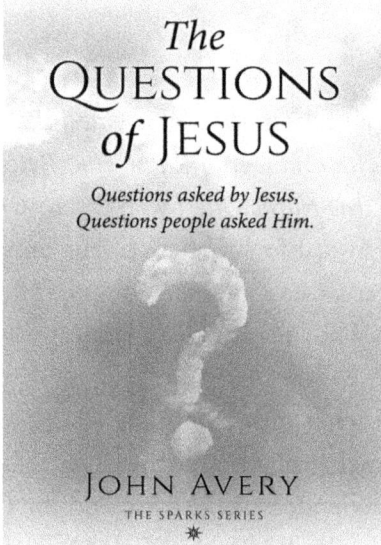

*Questions asked by Jesus,
Questions people asked Him.*

Available from Amazon,
www.NamesForGod.net, www.BibleMaturity.com/shop
and by ordering from major booksellers worldwide.

The
KINGDOM
of GOD

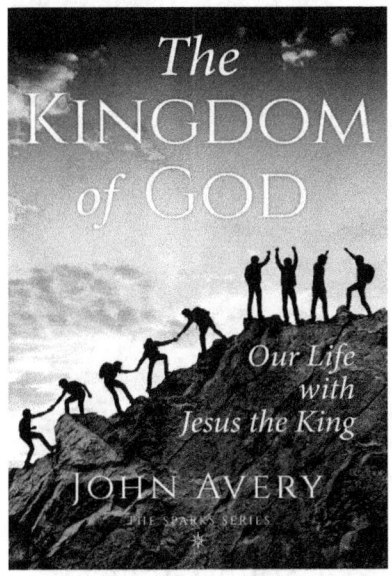

Our Life with Jesus the King

Available from Amazon,
www.NamesForGod.net, www.BibleMaturity.com/shop
and by ordering from major booksellers worldwide.

The NAME QUEST

A Study Guide for
The NAME QUEST

Both available from Amazon,
www.NamesForGod.net, www.BibleMaturity.com/shop
and by ordering from major booksellers worldwide.

**Watch for other and future compilations
in the Sparks Series in titles or on topics like:**

The Questions of Jesus
(Published October 2022)

The Kingdom of God
(Published March 2023)

Being like Jesus

Our Identity as Children of God

Talking to God

Faith in God

The Spirit of God

Following the Voice of God

Revival from God

Prophets of God

Names of God

Followers of Jesus

Kings of Israel
(David, Saul, and others)

Fathers of Faith
(Abraham, Jacob, and Moses)

Various other in-depth devotionals are at
www.BibleMaturity.com

THE SPARKS SERIES

www.ingramcontent.com/pod-product-compliance
Lightning Source LLC
Chambersburg PA
CBHW070439010526
44118CB00014B/2110